THIS BOOK BELONGS

THIS HOUSE PLANNER WILL HELP YOU STAY ORGANIZED,
AND KEEP ALL OF YOUR IMPORTANT INFORMATION IN ONE PLACE

IN THIS BOOK THERE ARE PAGES FOR FILLING OUT
HOME DETAILS LIKE;

- YEAR HOUSE WAS BUILT
- PURCHASE DATE & PRICE
- ADDRESS
- MORTGAGE PROVIDER
- MAJOR APPLIANCES EG; OVEN, SERIAL NO, WARRANTY, PRICE
- HOUSEHOLD BILLS

EACH ROOM HAS 6 SECTIONS FOR YOU TO FILL OUT,
INCLUDING;

- **INTERIOR DESIGN** - DIMENSIONS, INPUT IDEAS FOR FLOORING, CEILING, WALLS, TRIM, DOORS
- **LAYOUT PLAN** - DOTTED PAGE SO YOU CAN SKETCH YOUR IDEAL LAYOUT AND FLOOR PLAN
- **TO DO LIST** - INPUT TASKS YOU NEED TO DO FOR EACH ROOM, EG; CALL PLUMBER TO INSTALL KITCHEN TAP ETC
- **QUOTE PAGE** - INPUT WHAT JOB YOU NEED DONE, THE COMPANY, PRICE AND THOUGHTS ABOUT THEM
- **ITEMS PURCHASED** - ITEMS YOU HAVE BOUGHT FOR EACH ROOM, KEEP TABS ON YOUR BUDGET

ORDER OF CONTENTS

HOME DETAILS

HOUSEHOLD BILLS

MAJOR APPLIANCES

KITCHEN

LIVING ROOM

DINING ROOM

MASTER BEDROOM

BEDROOM 2

BEDROOM 3

BEDROOM 4

BEDROOM 5

BATHROOM 1

BATHROOM 2

BATHROOM 3

BATHROOM 4

ENTRANCE / HALLWAY

GARDEN

CUSTOM ROOMS

HOME DETAILS

ADDRESS	
YEAR HOUSE WAS BUILT	
PURCHASE DATE	
PURCHASE PRICE	
MORTGAGE PROVIDER	
OTHER DETAILS	

HOUSEHOLD BILLS

COST PER MONTH

BILL	PROVIDER	YEAR 1	YEAR 2	YEAR 3

MAJOR APPLIANCES

	ON MOVING IN
BRAND	
SUPPLIED BY	
DATE PURCHASED	
COST	
MODEL / SERIAL	
WARRANTY	
DIMENSIONS	
	REPLACEMENT
BRAND	
SUPPLIED BY	
DATE PURCHASED	
COST	
MODEL / SERIAL	
WARRANTY	
DIMENSIONS	

MAJOR APPLIANCES

	ON MOVING IN
BRAND	
SUPPLIED BY	
DATE PURCHASED	
COST	
MODEL / SERIAL	
WARRANTY	
DIMENSIONS	
	REPLACEMENT
BRAND	
SUPPLIED BY	
DATE PURCHASED	
COST	
MODEL / SERIAL	
WARRANTY	
DIMENSIONS	

MAJOR APPLIANCES

	ON MOVING IN
BRAND	
SUPPLIED BY	
DATE PURCHASED	
COST	
MODEL / SERIAL	
WARRANTY	
DIMENSIONS	
	REPLACEMENT
BRAND	
SUPPLIED BY	
DATE PURCHASED	
COST	
MODEL / SERIAL	
WARRANTY	
DIMENSIONS	

MAJOR APPLIANCES

	ON MOVING IN
BRAND	
SUPPLIED BY	
DATE PURCHASED	
COST	
MODEL / SERIAL	
WARRANTY	
DIMENSIONS	
	REPLACEMENT
BRAND	
SUPPLIED BY	
DATE PURCHASED	
COST	
MODEL / SERIAL	
WARRANTY	
DIMENSIONS	

MAJOR APPLIANCES

	ON MOVING IN
BRAND	
SUPPLIED BY	
DATE PURCHASED	
COST	
MODEL / SERIAL	
WARRANTY	
DIMENSIONS	
	REPLACEMENT
BRAND	
SUPPLIED BY	
DATE PURCHASED	
COST	
MODEL / SERIAL	
WARRANTY	
DIMENSIONS	

MAJOR APPLIANCES

	ON MOVING IN
BRAND	
SUPPLIED BY	
DATE PURCHASED	
COST	
MODEL / SERIAL	
WARRANTY	
DIMENSIONS	
	REPLACEMENT
BRAND	
SUPPLIED BY	
DATE PURCHASED	
COST	
MODEL / SERIAL	
WARRANTY	
DIMENSIONS	

MAJOR APPLIANCES

	ON MOVING IN
BRAND	
SUPPLIED BY	
DATE PURCHASED	
COST	
MODEL / SERIAL	
WARRANTY	
DIMENSIONS	
	REPLACEMENT
BRAND	
SUPPLIED BY	
DATE PURCHASED	
COST	
MODEL / SERIAL	
WARRANTY	
DIMENSIONS	

INTERIOR DESIGN PLAN

KITCHEN

DIMENSIONS _____

OF WINDOWS _____ # OF DOORS _____

WINDOW 1 SIZE _____ DOOR 1 _____

WINDOW 2 SIZE _____ DOOR 2 _____

WINDOW 3 SIZE _____ DOOR 3 _____

COLOR / STYLE _____

   WALLS _____

   FLOOR _____

   CEILING _____

   TRIM _____

   DOORS _____

NOTES / IDEAS

KITCHEN LAYOUT PLAN

KITCHEN TO DO LIST

TASK	FINISHED

KITCHEN QUOTES

DATE	COMPANY	SERVICE/JOB	PRICE	THOUGHTS

PURCHASED KITCHEN ITEMS

ITEM	SUPPLIER	COST
	TOTAL	

NOTES

INTERIOR DESIGN PLAN

LIVING ROOM

DIMENSIONS _____

OF WINDOWS _____ # OF DOORS _____

WINDOW 1 SIZE _____ DOOR 1 _____

WINDOW 2 SIZE _____ DOOR 2 _____

WINDOW 3 SIZE _____ DOOR 3 _____

COLOR / STYLE _____

    WALLS _____

    FLOOR _____

    CEILING _____

    TRIM _____

    DOORS _____

NOTES / IDEAS

LIVING ROOM PLAN

LIVING ROOM TO DO LIST

TASK	FINISHED

LIVING ROOM QUOTES

DATE	COMPANY	SERVICE/JOB	PRICE	THOUGHTS

PURCHASED LIVING ROOM ITEMS

ITEM	SUPPLIER	COST
	TOTAL	

NOTES

INTERIOR DESIGN PLAN

DINING ROOM

DIMENSIONS _____

\# OF WINDOWS _____ \# OF DOORS _____

WINDOW 1 SIZE _____ DOOR 1 _____

WINDOW 2 SIZE _____ DOOR 2 _____

WINDOW 3 SIZE _____ DOOR 3 _____

COLOR / STYLE _____

    WALLS _____

    FLOOR _____

    CEILING _____

    TRIM _____

    DOORS _____

NOTES / IDEAS

DINING ROOM PLAN

DINING ROOM TO DO LIST

TASK	FINISHED

DINING ROOM QUOTES

DATE	COMPANY	SERVICE/JOB	PRICE	THOUGHTS

PURCHASED DINING ROOM ITEMS

ITEM	SUPPLIER	COST
	TOTAL	

NOTES

INTERIOR DESIGN PLAN

MASTER BEDROOM

DIMENSIONS   _____

OF WINDOWS   _____   # OF DOORS   _____

WINDOW 1 SIZE   _____   DOOR 1   _____

WINDOW 2 SIZE   _____   DOOR 2   _____

WINDOW 3 SIZE   _____   DOOR 3   _____

COLOR / STYLE   _____

    WALLS   _____

    FLOOR   _____

    CEILING   _____

    TRIM   _____

    DOORS   _____

NOTES / IDEAS

MASTER BEDROOM PLAN

MASTER BEDROOM TO DO LIST

TASK	FINISHED

MASTER BEDROOM QUOTES

DATE	COMPANY	SERVICE/JOB	PRICE	THOUGHTS

PURCHASED MASTER BEDROOM ITEMS

ITEM	SUPPLIER	COST
	TOTAL	

NOTES

INTERIOR DESIGN PLAN

BEDROOM 2

DIMENSIONS _____

OF WINDOWS _____ # OF DOORS _____

WINDOW 1 SIZE _____ DOOR 1 _____

WINDOW 2 SIZE _____ DOOR 2 _____

WINDOW 3 SIZE _____ DOOR 3 _____

COLOR / STYLE _____

    WALLS _____

    FLOOR _____

    CEILING _____

    TRIM _____

    DOORS _____

NOTES / IDEAS

BEDROOM 2 PLAN

BEDROOM 2 TO DO LIST

TASK	FINISHED

BEDROOM 2 QUOTES

DATE	COMPANY	SERVICE/JOB	PRICE	THOUGHTS

PURCHASED BEDROOM 2 ITEMS

ITEM	SUPPLIER	COST
	TOTAL	

NOTES

INTERIOR DESIGN PLAN

BEDROOM 3

DIMENSIONS   _____

OF WINDOWS   _____   # OF DOORS   _____

WINDOW 1 SIZE   _____   DOOR 1   _____

WINDOW 2 SIZE   _____   DOOR 2   _____

WINDOW 3 SIZE   _____   DOOR 3   _____

COLOR / STYLE   _____

    WALLS   _____

    FLOOR   _____

    CEILING   _____

    TRIM   _____

    DOORS   _____

NOTES / IDEAS

BEDROOM 3 PLAN

BEDROOM 3 TO DO LIST

TASK	FINISHED

BEDROOM 3 QUOTES

DATE	COMPANY	SERVICE/JOB	PRICE	THOUGHTS

PURCHASED BEDROOM 3 ITEMS

ITEM	SUPPLIER	COST
	TOTAL	

NOTES

INTERIOR DESIGN PLAN

BEDROOM 4

DIMENSIONS _____

OF WINDOWS _____ # OF DOORS _____

WINDOW 1 SIZE _____ DOOR 1 _____

WINDOW 2 SIZE _____ DOOR 2 _____

WINDOW 3 SIZE _____ DOOR 3 _____

COLOR / STYLE _____

WALLS _____

FLOOR _____

CEILING _____

TRIM _____

DOORS _____

NOTES / IDEAS

BEDROOM 4 PLAN

BEDROOM 4 TO DO LIST

TASK	FINISHED

BEDROOM 4 QUOTES

DATE	COMPANY	SERVICE/JOB	PRICE	THOUGHTS

PURCHASED BEDROOM 4 ITEMS

ITEM	SUPPLIER	COST
	TOTAL	

NOTES

INTERIOR DESIGN PLAN

BEDROOM 5

DIMENSIONS _____

OF WINDOWS _____ # OF DOORS _____

WINDOW 1 SIZE _____ DOOR 1 _____

WINDOW 2 SIZE _____ DOOR 2 _____

WINDOW 3 SIZE _____ DOOR 3 _____

COLOR / STYLE _____

WALLS _____

FLOOR _____

CEILING _____

TRIM _____

DOORS _____

NOTES / IDEAS

BEDROOM 5 PLAN

BEDROOM 5 TO DO LIST

TASK	FINISHED

BEDROOM 5 QUOTES

DATE	COMPANY	SERVICE/JOB	PRICE	THOUGHTS

PURCHASED BEDROOM 5 ITEMS

ITEM	SUPPLIER	COST
	TOTAL	

NOTES

INTERIOR DESIGN PLAN

BATHROOM 1

DIMENSIONS _____

OF WINDOWS _____ # OF DOORS _____

WINDOW 1 SIZE _____ DOOR 1 _____

WINDOW 2 SIZE _____ DOOR 2 _____

WINDOW 3 SIZE _____ DOOR 3 _____

COLOR / STYLE _____

WALLS _____

FLOOR _____

CEILING _____

TRIM _____

DOORS _____

NOTES / IDEAS

BATHROOM I PLAN

BATHROOM I TO DO LIST

TASK	FINISHED

BATHROOM I QUOTES

DATE	COMPANY	SERVICE/JOB	PRICE	THOUGHTS

PURCHASED BATHROOM I ITEMS

ITEM	SUPPLIER	COST
	TOTAL	

NOTES

INTERIOR DESIGN PLAN

BATHROOM 2

DIMENSIONS _____

OF WINDOWS _____ # OF DOORS _____

WINDOW 1 SIZE _____ DOOR 1 _____

WINDOW 2 SIZE _____ DOOR 2 _____

WINDOW 3 SIZE _____ DOOR 3 _____

COLOR / STYLE _____

    WALLS _____

    FLOOR _____

    CEILING _____

    TRIM _____

    DOORS _____

NOTES / IDEAS

BATHROOM 2 PLAN

BATHROOM 2 TO DO LIST

TASK	FINISHED

BATHROOM 2 QUOTES

DATE	COMPANY	SERVICE/JOB	PRICE	THOUGHTS

PURCHASED BATHROOM 2 ITEMS

ITEM	SUPPLIER	COST
	TOTAL	

NOTES

INTERIOR DESIGN PLAN

BATHROOM 3

DIMENSIONS _____

OF WINDOWS _____ # OF DOORS _____

WINDOW 1 SIZE _____ DOOR 1 _____

WINDOW 2 SIZE _____ DOOR 2 _____

WINDOW 3 SIZE _____ DOOR 3 _____

COLOR / STYLE _____

    WALLS _____

    FLOOR _____

    CEILING _____

    TRIM _____

    DOORS _____

NOTES / IDEAS

BATHROOM 3 PLAN

BATHROOM 3 TO DO LIST

TASK	FINISHED

BATHROOM 3 QUOTES

DATE	COMPANY	SERVICE/JOB	PRICE	THOUGHTS

PURCHASED BATHROOM 3 ITEMS

ITEM	SUPPLIER	COST
	TOTAL	

NOTES

INTERIOR DESIGN PLAN

BATHROOM 4

DIMENSIONS _____

OF WINDOWS _____ # OF DOORS _____

WINDOW 1 SIZE _____ DOOR 1 _____

WINDOW 2 SIZE _____ DOOR 2 _____

WINDOW 3 SIZE _____ DOOR 3 _____

COLOR / STYLE _____

   WALLS _____

   FLOOR _____

   CEILING _____

   TRIM _____

   DOORS _____

NOTES / IDEAS

BATHROOM 4 PLAN

BATHROOM 4 TO DO LIST

TASK	FINISHED

BATHROOM 4 QUOTES

DATE	COMPANY	SERVICE/JOB	PRICE	THOUGHTS

PURCHASED BATHROOM 4 ITEMS

ITEM	SUPPLIER	COST
	TOTAL	

NOTES

INTERIOR DESIGN PLAN

ENTRANCE / HALLWAY

DIMENSIONS _____

OF WINDOWS _____ # OF DOORS _____

WINDOW 1 SIZE _____ DOOR 1 _____

WINDOW 2 SIZE _____ DOOR 2 _____

WINDOW 3 SIZE _____ DOOR 3 _____

COLOR / STYLE _____

   WALLS _____

   FLOOR _____

   CEILING _____

   TRIM _____

   DOORS _____

NOTES / IDEAS

ENTRANCE / HALLWAY PLAN

ENTRANCE / HALLWAY TO DO LIST

TASK	FINISHED

ENTRANCE / HALLWAY QUOTES

DATE	COMPANY	SERVICE/JOB	PRICE	THOUGHTS

PURCHASED ENTRANCE / HALLWAY ITEMS

ITEM	SUPPLIER	COST
	TOTAL	

NOTES

DESIGN PLAN

GARDEN

DIMENSIONS _____

_____   _____

_____   _____

_____   _____

_____   _____

COLOR / STYLE _____

FENCE _____

GROUND _____

LIGHTING _____

SEATING _____

DECKING _____

NOTES / IDEAS

GARDEN PLAN

GARDEN TO DO LIST

TASK	FINISHED

GARDEN QUOTES

DATE	COMPANY	SERVICE/JOB	PRICE	THOUGHTS

PURCHASED GARDEN ITEMS

ITEM	SUPPLIER	COST
	TOTAL	

NOTES

INTERIOR DESIGN PLAN

_____

DIMENSIONS _____

OF WINDOWS _____ # OF DOORS _____

WINDOW 1 SIZE _____ DOOR 1 _____

WINDOW 2 SIZE _____ DOOR 2 _____

WINDOW 3 SIZE _____ DOOR 3 _____

COLOR / STYLE _____

   WALLS _____

   FLOOR _____

   CEILING _____

   TRIM _____

   DOORS _____

NOTES / IDEAS

_____ PLAN

_____ TO DO LIST

TASK	FINISHED

_____ QUOTES

DATE	COMPANY	SERVICE/JOB	PRICE	THOUGHTS

PURCHASED _____ ITEMS

ITEM	SUPPLIER	COST
	TOTAL	

NOTES

INTERIOR DESIGN PLAN

_____

DIMENSIONS _____

OF WINDOWS _____ # OF DOORS _____

WINDOW 1 SIZE _____ DOOR 1 _____

WINDOW 2 SIZE _____ DOOR 2 _____

WINDOW 3 SIZE _____ DOOR 3 _____

COLOR / STYLE _____

  WALLS _____

  FLOOR _____

  CEILING _____

  TRIM _____

  DOORS _____

NOTES / IDEAS

_____ PLAN

_____ TO DO LIST

TASK	FINISHED

_____ QUOTES

DATE	COMPANY	SERVICE/JOB	PRICE	THOUGHTS

PURCHASED _____ ITEMS

ITEM	SUPPLIER	COST
	TOTAL	

NOTES

INTERIOR DESIGN PLAN

_____

DIMENSIONS   _____

OF WINDOWS   _____   # OF DOORS   _____

WINDOW 1 SIZE   _____   DOOR 1   _____

WINDOW 2 SIZE   _____   DOOR 2   _____

WINDOW 3 SIZE   _____   DOOR 3   _____

COLOR / STYLE   _____

   WALLS   _____

   FLOOR   _____

   CEILING   _____

   TRIM   _____

   DOORS   _____

NOTES / IDEAS

_____ PLAN

_____ TO DO LIST

TASK	FINISHED

_____ QUOTES

DATE	COMPANY	SERVICE/JOB	PRICE	THOUGHTS

PURCHASED _____ ITEMS

ITEM	SUPPLIER	COST
	TOTAL	

NOTES

INTERIOR DESIGN PLAN

_____

DIMENSIONS _____

OF WINDOWS _____ # OF DOORS _____

WINDOW 1 SIZE _____ DOOR 1 _____

WINDOW 2 SIZE _____ DOOR 2 _____

WINDOW 3 SIZE _____ DOOR 3 _____

COLOR / STYLE _____

WALLS _____

FLOOR _____

CEILING _____

TRIM _____

DOORS _____

NOTES / IDEAS

_____ PLAN

_____ TO DO LIST

TASK	FINISHED

_____ QUOTES

DATE	COMPANY	SERVICE/JOB	PRICE	THOUGHTS

PURCHASED _____ ITEMS

ITEM	SUPPLIER	COST
	TOTAL	

NOTES

Printed in Great Britain
by Amazon